Bernie Sparks

&

Rocky the Rocket

On

BONFIRE NIGHT

Remember, Remember
The 5th of November,
Gunpowder, Treason
& Plot,
I See No Reason Why
Gunpowder Treason,
Should Ever Be Forgot

Bonfire night is an annual event that is dedicated to fireworks, bonfires and celebrations with friends and family. Each year bonfire night is traditionally celebrated on the 5th November in England to mark the date that Guy Fawkes attempted to ignite gunpowder beneath the House of Lords in London.

Bonfire night is a fun celebration to be enjoyed, but you must remember to stay safe. So here to tell you how to be safe are Bernie sparks and his firework friend Rocky the Rocket.

Keep Pets Indoors

"OK I'll do that straight away. Will we have sparklers at the bonfire, I love sparklers Bernie?"

"I like them too Rocky, but mom says we have to be careful with sparklers. Mom said that we need to wear gloves when we are holding a sparkler and that we should hold the sparkler at arm's length so that we don't get hurt."

"What do we do when we are finished with the sparklers Bernie?"

"Well Mom said that, when the sparkler goes out, we must not touch it, as they get very hot. She said that we need to put the hot end of the sparkler into a cold bucket of water so that it can cool down, and so that we don't get burnt."

"Can I give a sparkler to my young sister as well Bernie?"

"No, sorry Rocky, mom said that really young children shouldn't hold sparklers, as they might hurt themselves as they are too young to use them properly."

Don't Give Sparklers to Young Children

Only Adults Can Light Fireworks

"Where can we watch the fireworks Bernie?"

"Well Rocky, fireworks are beautiful and they are full of colours, and people of any age are allowed to watch them shoot up into the sky. But, mom says that we need to stand well back away from where the adults are lighting the fireworks, so that we can stay safe and so that the fireworks can't hurt us."

In the night-time darkness,

In the night-time cold,

Did you spot a Catherine wheel

Raining showers of gold?

Did you watch a rocket

Go zoom into the sky?

And hear a bonfire crackle

As the sparks lit up the guy?

In the night-time darkness,

In the night-time cold,

Did you clutch a sparkler

As it scattered stars of gold?

Catherine Wheel

More Books for Kids

Squirts Lost Her Spots

Squirt and the Polar Bears

Squirt and the Island Treasure

Squirt and the Christmas Adventure

Midnight Monsters

Large Larry

The Opticlops

Printed in Great Britain
by Amazon